Fabulous Female Athletes

by Peggy Bresnick Kendler

Editorial Offices: Glenview, Illinois • Parsippany, New Jersey • New York, New York
Sales Offices: Needham, Massachusetts • Duluth, Georgia • Glenview, Illinois
Coppell, Texas • Ontario, California • Mesa, Arizona

ISBN: 0-328-13428-7

Women and Sports

Years ago, women were not allowed to play the same sports as men. Girls had fewer chances to play organized sports than boys. It was not fair that girls were not treated the same.

However, many girls liked to play the same sports as boys. They liked to play baseball, basketball, golf, and soccer. Many girls liked to compete and to win and did not want to sit on the sidelines.

Today females have many chances to play the same sports that males do. They can play in school, in college, on local teams, and as professionals. Women now have opportunities to play sports because a long time ago a few brave women fought hard for that chance.

These young female athletes are ready to play baseball.

Opportunities Then and Now

Thousands of years ago, when the Olympic Games began in ancient Greece, only men were allowed to compete. Women could only play in unofficial games.

Women first played in the Olympic Games in 1900, in Paris, France. Only 22 female athletes out of 997 total athletes competed in these games. Women competed in five sports: tennis, sailing, golf, equestrian events, and croquet.

Many more women participate in the Olympic Games today. In the 2000 Olympics, there were 4,069 female athletes competing in 25 different sports.

In 1900 women were permitted to participate in the Olympic Games. Charlotte Cooper was the first woman to win an Olympic title in Paris, France.

An Early Female Athlete

A championship golfer as well as a track and field star, Mildred Didrikson Zaharias was one of the most famous early women athletes in the United States. She was known as "Babe" because she could hit a baseball like Babe Ruth.

Babe Didrikson Zaharias was good at many different sports. Although she was a talented softball and basketball player, Babe was a great all-around athlete.

In 1932 Babe won several important track and field events. She even went to the Olympics that year where she won gold medals in the javelin throw and the 80-meter hurdles and a silver medal for the high jump.

In 1934 Babe began another sports career, playing on the amateur golf tour. She won many major golf tournaments between 1946 and 1954.

A Professional All-Girl Baseball League

In 1943 a group of women joined together and made a name for themselves in sports. They were called the All-American Girls Professional Baseball League. It was the nation's first all-female professional baseball league.

At the time, many men in the United States were fighting overseas in World War II. In the United States, women worked in jobs to support the war.

Baseball was a popular sport at that time, and people still wanted to watch games. So women began to play professional baseball while the men were at war. A few hundred women who liked to play softball and were very good at it signed up to play professional baseball.

The All-American Girls Professional Baseball League in 1945

6

The All-American Girls Professional Baseball League replaced the men's league, keeping baseball stadiums filled while the men were away. Some of the women on the first teams were young, and some were older and had families of their own. The youngest player was only fifteen and needed her mother's permission to join a team!

Even though these women were tough competitors, the league organizers wanted them to look feminine on the field. They didn't wear the typical uniform of pants and a baseball jersey. They played in dresses instead and wore makeup for every game.

After the war was over, the men's professional baseball leagues began again. Few people went to see the women's games. The women's league went on for nearly nine more years before ending in 1954.

Members of the Kenosha Comets during a 1943 practice

The World's Fastest Women

Wilma Rudolph

Some athletes like to compete on the track, but nobody knew that Wilma Rudolph would turn out to be such a fast runner! When Wilma was born in 1940, she weighed just $4\frac{1}{2}$ pounds. She suffered from polio as a child. This disease left her left leg and foot weak and twisted. Doctors thought she would never walk normally again.

Wilma was a determined girl. She worked with many doctors, and her family helped her to try to make her leg strong. When she was twelve, Wilma could walk and even run. The doctors **marveled** at Wilma's **unbelievable** recovery. She surprised everyone and became an athlete.

One of the world's greatest female track stars, Wilma Rudolph won three gold medals in the 1960 Olympic Games in Rome, Italy.

Officials unveil a Wilma Rudolph commemorative U.S. postage stamp in her hometown of Clarksville, Tennessee, in 2004.

By the time Wilma got to high school, her legs were strong. She became one of the best basketball players in the state. Then she joined the track and field team and became a star. She found out how much she loved to run.

Wilma went to the Olympic Games in 1956 when she was sixteen. She won a bronze medal in the relay race. At the 1960 Olympics, Wilma became the first American woman to win three gold medals in one Olympics, all in running.

Not only did Wilma win her fight against an illness that could have left her crippled, she became a champion. She made it easier for women to compete in track and field events, which were once only for men.

Florence Griffith Joyner

Wilma Rudolph inspired many young female athletes. African American women like Florence Griffith Joyner looked up to her. Florence was the next female athlete to win three gold medals in one Olympics.

In her career, Florence set two world records, for the 100-meter dash and the 200-meter dash. She won both races at the 1988 Olympics. She ran so fast that she left the world **speechless.**

Florence Griffith Joyner

Jackie Joyner-Kersee

Another great African American athlete was Florence's sister-in-law, Jackie Joyner-Kersee. Jackie was a track and field champion best known for the heptathlon, a competition in which the athletes compete in seven track and field events. To win the heptathlon, Jackie had to be fast, strong, and full of energy. Jackie won six Olympic medals from 1984 to 1996. Three were in heptathlon events.

Jackie Joyner-Kersee

Taking Tennis to the Next Level

Some athletes play their best on the tennis court. Althea Gibson played in amateur tournaments as a young adult before she became a professional tennis player. She won eleven major tennis titles between 1956 and 1958.

Althea Gibson was a great female tennis star. She was also the first African American person to win competitive tennis tournaments, including Wimbledon and the U.S. Open. She paved the way for future African American athletes, male and female, to compete in a sport that was once open only to white people.

Althea Gibson was the first African American woman to win a championship at a major tennis tournament.

Billie Jean King's tennis skills and her confidence on the court still influence many female tennis stars today, including Venus and Serena Williams.

Billie Jean King also has a success story. Billie Jean took up tennis at age eleven in 1954. She was a powerful athlete who **swatted** the ball over the net with great force. She later became one of the world's greatest tennis players.

Billie Jean King also spoke out for the rights of women to earn the same pay as men in tennis and other sports. She got the U.S. Open to award equal prizes to men and women. She also helped set up a professional women's tennis tour.

Women on the Basketball Court

Some female athletes do well on the basketball court. In the mid-1990s, women's basketball became popular, but there was no basketball league just for female players. In 1996 the Women's National Basketball Association, the WNBA, began.

Women who had been star basketball players in high school and college showed great interest in joining the new teams. The women formed eight professional teams by the first game in June 1997.

Before 1996, there was no women's professional basketball league.

Most of the game rules for the WNBA are similar to the men's league, the NBA. For instance, a player who pushes into another player has **fouled** her, and players are not allowed to hang on the basketball net or **rim.** The game itself is the same. The goal is always to put the ball in the **hoop.**

WNBA games are played during the summer. During the first season of WNBA play in 1997, more than fifty million people watched the games on television.

Today there are sixteen teams in the WNBA. In 2002 there were 176 women playing professional basketball for the WNBA.

Lisa Leslie was one of the first female athletes to sign on to a WNBA team.

Young girls play soccer in Mill Valley, California.

An all-girl basketball team competes on an indoor court.

An Equal Opportunity for All

More than thirty years ago, girls did not play the same sports in school as boys. They did not always have the same sports equipment, training, or playing fields that the boys had in the same school. Many girls could not to play the sports that they liked.

In 1972 the U.S. government passed a law called Title IX. This law bans gender discrimination in colleges that get money from the U.S. government. One result of Title IX is that women now have the same chance as men to play and do well in college sports.

Since the law was passed, more and more girls have decided to play sports in school. Many of these girls have gone on to careers in sports. Some have even gone on to the Olympics or become professional sports stars. If this law had never been created, some of the sports champions we know today might never have had a chance to play.

Women Sports Stars Today

Women have not always had an easy time playing sports. But because of some determined female athletes, there are more chances for girls to play sports today than ever before.

Millions of girls compete in sports at all levels, from youth leagues to professional play. Women's tennis, golf, soccer, and basketball are growing more popular all the time.

Girls are getting better training. Today they are treated better on the court, field, and track than they were at any other time in history. Professional sports women are paid well for their performances—something that did not happen many years ago.

Venus and Serena Williams, terrific at tennis

Nancy Lopez, golfing great

Women today compete professionally because of the great women athletes who came before them. Those women fought for the chance to compete and for the chance to shine in the sports they played.

The journey of women athletes was not always easy. Those who found a way to form teams and compete professionally were brave women. They paved the way for female athletes of today and tomorrow.

Mia Hamm,
soccer superstar

Glossary

amateur *adj.* for or by a person who does something for pleasure, not for money or profession.

fouled *v.* made an unfair play against.

hoop *n.* ring; round, flat band.

jersey *n.* shirt that is pulled over the head made of soft knitted cloth.

marveled *v.* filled with wonder; astonished.

rim *n.* an edge, border, or margin on or around anything.

speechless *adj.* not able to talk.

swatted *v.* hit sharply or violently.

unbelievable *adj.* incredible; hard to think of as true or real.